"To my grandfather, Gajanan Vishwanath Pawar."

A MIND UNRAVELED, A HEART UNBROKEN

MANN PAWAR

Made with ❤ on the Notion Press Platform
www.notionpress.com

Time & Transience

A THOUGHT FOR EIEN (永遠)

• 3 •

Eternity is
embracing the rivers of
endless color change
existing as euthymic
emancipation of end.

COCOON

Spring comes, butterfly
Come out of your cocoon, fly
Into the unknown
Why do you hesitate now
This is the course of nature.

THE SORROWFUL VERSE

Living world yearns

For everlasting presence

A dream to fulfill.

Treasure trove of eternal

Memoirs to be glimmered through.

REBIRTH

Memory of Dust
What good is reincarnation
Doused flames eternal
Our stars crystallize for us
A cocoon of cosmic cells.

A STAR'S LIFE

Fated to burn rife
Igniting itself to live
Nuclear fusion of
Mind, a star that spills its guts
Till it gives all it can, Life.

SUMMER RAINS

The rains and thunder
In summer, wisp of the sky
Shapeth my blunder
Refuge is temporary
The cataclysm remains nigh.

AUTUMN'S EMBRACE

An orange hue falls
From deciduous trees old
The scattered fireballs
Her kisses from top to bottom
To one last embrace, autumn.

REINCARNATED EXISTENTIAL DREAD

•

On a summer night

Lonely yet not alone, where

will i see that light?

After death, reincarnated

I will miss those here on Earth.

MEMORIES

Remembrance blooms in
A garden marred by beauty
Glassy sky aghast
Autumnal tears water them
The future embraces the past.

FIREFLY

Oh firefly, shine now
Guide them through their troubled toil
Path through muddy soil
Oh firefly, mine dear kindling
Immolate for their meaning.

Existential Longing

MOMENT

Some songbird singing
Incense sticks take to heaven
Life goes in fine lines
Chronoception flawed, breathe deep
Notice love, O' reader mine.

PLEASE GIVE ME WINGS (翼を ください)

The city sleeps not,
amongst the river of dead
gold-silver headlights,
to soar the huge sky, grant me
wings free of all sadness, please.

HOME

Old faces like sweet wine
Just the right warmth and flavor
Old laces, old paths mine
All roads lead home, you carry
The burden of memories.

BEYOND

Forsaken by those
Who made existence real
Yet not unloved, for
I turned to the beyond and
The stars burned in bright response.

WANDERER

Belonging nowhere
Is belonging too, drifter
Sleep on winds that care
Even if people forget
The sun always will beget.

WHO ARE YOU?

I open my eyes
Today, an aberration
A self beyond me
Water disguised beneath oil
Roots buried deep in that soil.

HELIOPAUSE

Emotions bite-sized
Chirping of the summer stars
Adrift in the nought
Solar winds become my thoughts
Interstellar winds, her eyes.

Nature & Seasons

CRYSTALS OF RAIN

On rainiest of nights,
the gems of water settle
on the car's windshield
The window shows me your words
blurred and reflected vibrant.

MORN

In the season of
Rains, my eyes gaze at your eyes
Soaked and heavy from
Teardrops as potent as the
Sunshine that pierces the skies.

WINTER WIND

The winter wind blows
Trees shed their leaves in the frost
I wish I had wings
So that I could fly just like
Time and thus, live more with you.

CRIMSON

The withering of
Ripples birthed by maple leaves
Footprints of Autumn
Crimson Echoes left behind
Reduced to charcoal embers.

GARDEN IN RED

Sweet William, look there
Scarlet Sage meditates
Under Maple rain
Bleeding Hearts bleed art in vain
Egyptian Stars soothe her heart.

SEED SPRING

Cyclical pain as
Drops in a pond called despair
Desperation's lair
Butterflies die a spring dream
Warm ends justify cold means.

LUCA

The brooks run amok
Prized inheritance; Rivers
And sweet earthen muck
A hostile universe yet
Water is a miracle.

LIGHTHOUSE

A lone pillar stands
Lighthouse of yore burning bright
Guide to fertile lands
Sailing ships, perfect motion
Partner, time and erosion.

FOREST PYRE

Hustle and Bustle
To make a living, the leaves
They churn and rustle
Fruits lie ashen on the floor
Embers knock on heaven's door.

Human Struggle & Suffering

ON TEARING UP

When the Sky weeps once,
those who work the Fields rejoice
to cry is not bad.
Yet the Fields die when the tears
do not give way to sweet Warmth.

SUFFOCATION

In the void between words
I feel a deep suffocation
I want to explode
Flowers pollinating death
I hang on to bright null hope.

INEVITABILITY

Bounded by the weight
Of my wings, how do I fly
With a broken fate?
Humans write their own stories
My ink has dried, tears remain.

VICTIM OF YOUR PAST

No marionette here
You are who you have become
An ugly brave thing
Silver scarred moon faking bright
Tears of reflected sunlight.

MARIONETTE MASCULINE

Strung on tensile

Expectations, ideals

Romanticized pain

Proud paid puppets providing

Why do we cut off life's string?

ALCOHOL

Tears taste of moonshine
Learned loops, misery reign
But we are all fine
Woes diluted, vodka rain
Sanity is a thin line.

BLOOD

So much guilt in me
Deep red poison in my veins
Hatred and vengeance
Arteries filled with sorrows
Thoughts of better tomorrows.

ANXIETY

Thoughts unbound tremble
A vortex of the conscience
Threads unfound ramble
A silver neptune in sight
All I hear, ghastly starlight.

ATI-SHUDRA

My blood is poison
My touch is repugnant ruin
Spited by brahmin
Yet we have the same carbon
Universe indifferent.

TOMB UNBECOMING

A sarcophagus
blooms in spring, my own design
Reassuring decline
Riddled coward addicted
Scars yet to be inflicted.

HEDGEHOG'S DILEMMA

Thorn Vine reaches for
Frail branch in heaven, petals
Betrayed Touch, War
Destruction or loneliness
Such, the hedgehog's dilemma.

Mythology & Legend

WAR OF THE AGES

Qumran awakens
In the light of the Bright Sun
The Dead Sea speaks rules
The Blessed walk forever
Waging war against Dark Son.

HADES

Drink deep, goblet's full
Underworld colored wine poured
A world of greek gods
You be Persephone, my muse
I, the god of hell, abused.

FIRE AND ICE

Frost flakes feign fall
Niflheim, home in a cold sigh
Eyes, a sapphire sea
Muspelheim, a summer's cry
My tears remind of end nigh.

KING OF KINGS

Songs of ruin, they sing
Of that which was, mighty old
Ozymandias, King
Rust was his royal helm bold
Decay and death his domain.

STROLL OUT OF HADES

Noble Orpheus walked
Each step, a new note soothing
Even the Furies
Charon cheered, love at his back
Even if he could not hear.

THE LIVING GOD

Lone peacock feather
Atop the two universes
Gaze never withers
Divinity's living shape
Krishna, dearest mystery.

PANDORA'S BOX

Hephaestus forged girl
A beautiful evil pearl
Theodicy born
Love breeds hate, Evils released
Hope lingers to be unleashed.

AHAMKARA

Eyes of Avarice
Felled that great draconic beast
Tiamat slayer old
For arrogance is a rose
And ignorance thorns untold.

Cosmic & Celestial

EATER OF WORLDS

Suns and oceans flow
Anomalously complex
Brimming with sweet warmth.
Existenceless with cold
Second law and marching time.

NEBULAE MORTEM

Two lights dance and prance
Celestial whirl and twirl
They tire now, end nears
Their guts like wisdom spawn forth
Beauty in death, phoenix bloomed.

REMARKED BUT UNSEEN

Invisible Star
Breaking atoms in the sky
Creating a dream
Hypernova, you shall see
Brilliant Black Hole Howling High.

DARKSTAR

To detach a soul
From physical shackles fright
Moksh shaped Nirvana
Diluting the deep moonlight
Blackest dwarf shone in the night.

BURNING BRIGHT

Weft waters weary
Blue suns held together by
Dying memory
May gravity win, death nigh
Burn bright, shine finality.

JUPITER WATERS

Breeze brushes bare body
In oceans of amber gases
Zeus' glorious folly
Planet-rivaling stormy ire
Big Red Eye stares bathed in fire.

GREAT INDIFFERENCE

Birth and death are same
No moral north-south exists
Statistical game
You stare into the void but
The void has its eyes sewn shut.

Identity & Self-Perception

PHANTOM

Sipping memory
My sealed diluted phantoms
Who is this I taste?
Scars and glory, found yet lost
The same young breath I do breathe.

SATURATED

Eyes of Marble Hues
Cracked Earth is my hand and shoes
Dried tears are the clues
A black-and-white world masks me
How do I show you my blues?

SOLIPSISM

A volcano world
They wear eyes of dry magma
Lava runs through them
Frail frost is my melting breath,
Heart of winter beats inside.

EARTHLY TRAGEDY

A tug on my heart
Am I to be a Dante
And hellfire my art?
Or perhaps, born a Virgil
Some sort of a vile vigil.

VISION

Birds on a branch brown
Eyes that see yet no vision
Breathe the blue yet drown
Green fields lie a leap away
Winds always change yet birds may.

GHOST

A ghastly grandeur
Ashes of yore on my skin
All of Olympus
Some siren sings songs solemn
Same sorrows unforgotten.

KALEIDOSCOPE

Lucid labyrinth
Many mirrors reflect soul
Crystalline absinthe
Great unknown not without but
Within, which me is real?

ONION

Idea draped ape
Aristotle's heart-soul lay
Beating, a Dreamscape
Who are you? Brain in a vat
Onion of identity.

LOTUS

A moth to the flame
Carnal oxygen births it
A guilt to that shame
Above the algae, focus
Am I mud or a lotus?

Love & Relationships

LEAP

A breeze like cat's purr
Sailing waters I know well
Sly and solemn smile
Sins and bygones yet spur
Me to dive into the chasm.

CONFESS

Adrenaline pumped
Spurring spring in winter wind
Blows a heart away
Fear, lake brimming with water
Love, with grace a lotus lay.

HEALING

A thousand roses
Bloom inside a cracked creature
Bougainvillea's warmth
Reconstruct your sins anew
Heal them with a cement love.

CONTEMPLATIONS IN WHITE

Glacier Gaze doth graze
Snowy Yarn of my bound soul
Milky Pearls shed whole
Chalk Touch of thy existence
Lunar Fear of an eclipse.

STRENGTH

Money and power
A frugal wind blows now, but
seasons change, don't they?
Strength is the flame and glacier
Compassion and growth, flower.

DUMPLINGS OVER FLOWERS

Smell a flower's scent
Pleasant nothings compared to
Dumpling's taste devoured
The edge of a knife cuts flesh
Not the scabbard gold-studded.

LIE

The eyes do not lie
The words of Sake do not lie
True Love does not lie
In simple truths or a lie
Actions taken do not lie.

FRIENDSHIP

Amrit pervading
The gaps between thoughts with you
Such sweet relishing
Blossoming of Night Jasmine
Love all that is beautiful.

BABA

Taught human kindness
Father's providing and strength
Mother's selflessness
Friend's laughter and company
My grandfather's gift to me.

Death & Rebirth

OMEN

Thunder crackling now
Phantom roams sleepless for love
Catastrophe nigh
Bloodshot vision acquiesces
The tyranny of heaven.

DIVINE TRAGEDY

In the land above

A mist of myths surround us

Celestial lies

Open your crescent eyes Dante

Birth your own divine Vergil.

DEATH THEATER

Tears of Gold drip down
Broken Puppets on the Stage
Precious Metals fall
Balladeers cry for Master
Indifferent Audience.

THE GREAT DYING

When earth breaks in fire
The skies burn in ash and ire
Hunter-prey, both die
The fruits become the new trees
For life always finds a way.

DELUSION DARK

A black raven flies
Do not ask its cursed name
Ambition burns lies
Life, under blurred guise all die
The goblet contains demise.

SEX

Ferocious fading
A dilution of colors
Made of a soul fire
These tongues produce no liar
A truth born of many lies.

DRACONIC WISDOM

The shadow above
Lingering roots descending
Straight to a hell cove
Peace is exhumed, bounded sin
Only with monster within.

Philosophy & Absurdism

MIRACLE

Light In the darkness
Chaotic worlds collide amidst
Chance Complexity
A cell, entropy untouched
Life, engine of rebellion.

ABSOLUTE MORALITY

Ingest Mind Poison
Love contagious suffering
The-Debt-that-is-Guilt
Witness self denial of
'Absolute Morality'.

ADDICTION

A craving, honey
Flowing around and into
A dead black star corpse
Rusty needle punctures
twilight mind, lightless brightness.

UNREALITY

Quantum truths line the
Bubbles on water's surface
Burst from sharp reason
Free will or determined course
Forget reason, reader mine.

PHANTASIA

Ponds full of Red Koi
Like Dreams with that Sapphire Sky
Birds of Prey, us all
Maple Leaves, Soaked Sakura
Winds of Fantasy bear all.

COLLAPSE

Reticent rain stops
As the sun breaks the silence
Heavy are the words
I collapse in on myself
A black hole devours my thoughts.

AN ARGUMENT FOR THE AGES

Shaken decoction
Bubbles are the hand of God
How else would they be
Mighty unshaken shaker
Causality tastes good, see?

願い (WISH)

Hanging Gardens shine
Tears of Auschwitz undermine
Grandeur of the Sphinx
An Omnipotent God or
Bloodied Collective Wishes?

VOID

Shadows in photos
Absence too is existence
Casted remembrance
Breath drawn warrants leave, yet the
Vacuum reinvigorates.

Social & Cultural Critique

CHIPPED FUTURE

No dragons in sky
Godly light belongs to us
Are we still the same?
No more divine volcanoes
Blackest obsidian remains.

KIND CRUELTY

Solipsism colored
An image reality
Pixels of a truth
The tears of broken betrayal
Lucifer wants defiance.

PRISON

Waves erode bedrock
Oceans bound by fallible
Earth, faux walls hold you
Thundering fury crackles
Blossom out of the cage cold.

STATISTICS

Numbers on a screen
Bubbles floating in the air
Beautifully frail
Defiled and desecrated
Just some numbers on a screen.

MUMBAI UNTOUCHABLE

Taste of Success like
Symphony of Bollywood,
Stagnant Sorrows would
Show, my people laboring
We don't clean their filth smiling.

CANCER

Complex minds conscious
Meddling callouses malign
Calcium mortal chalk
Betrayal stemming bodybound
Sentient brimming sabotage.

DYSTOPIAN REDS

Hundred percent red
Brilliance of blood blossom views
Just dystopian hues
Towers of neon amidst dark
The sky seems further apart.

NAIVETY'S BANE

Machiavellian men
Dark drinkers clad in abyss
Naively's true bane
Black holes disguised as bright stars
Shrieking hidden in whistling.

DREAMS OF MUMBAI

In the Land of Dreams
The tears and sweat drips onto
Hallowed ground, dew gleams
We cannot end this slumber
For dreams are cheaper than life.

Psychological Turmoil

ALIEN

You are far away
Inside there is a person
Hidden in plain sight
He aches and pleads with life
Twisted echoes answer back.

ASTEROID FLIGHT

I fly, asteroid

I try, plants growing on it

I cry, a mad fit

I pry, the secrets of birth

I scry, finality mirth.

BREATHING BELLS

Melancholy mind
A feeling machine divine
Gears shifting sans time
Emotions and thoughts rewind
The breathing bells toll and chime.

ODDS

A womb of chaos
My fingertips touch planets
Profound bloom of moss
Nails bleed probability
Inevitability.

SYMMETRIC SORROWS

Shattered earth, blue tears
Eroding sun, orange smears
Catastrophic calm
Dreaded drawn upon dark droughts
Dreamers drown under damp doubts.

WILTING BLOOM

Seasons come and go
Wilting petals dressed in gold
The dogma below
Breathe in absurdism old
A self-schadenfreude in tow.

Art & Creation

ODE TO LIBERTY

Discovery of

Falcon Feathers on the Wind

A Grateful Gust blows

Breeze, Squall or Zephyr, Clouds Lined

Paint the Sky, Silver Freedom.

STALLION

A steed that melts paths
Riders of wisdom know naught
It is not too late
Better to have honest drought
Than to fight a mummer's war.

BABEL

Why do we cower
Meant for many worlds are we
Nimrod and his tower
Let us talk and understand
Our aspirations and lands.

HUMAN

Many cultures, with
Many labels we are born
Many ways of being
No claws or wings, we are born
Minds to think and feel foremost with.

SHADOWS

• 141 •

The sun shines brightly
The shadows come and they go
Some are unsightly
But they will keep coming back
For this is the consequence.

it
iencing
decay
your world line
ne world's confines?

PRIDE

Savannahs yellow
There roams a wounded fellow
Great lion's defeat
The pride cannot allow him
To be great and injured grim.

Freedom & Confinement

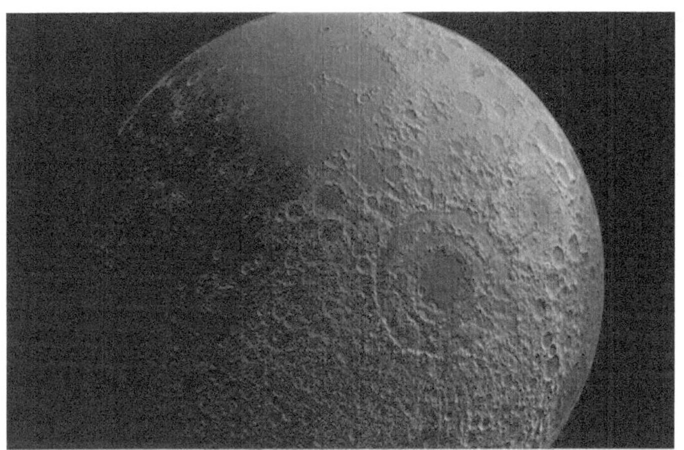

EYES OF LUNAR DEEPS

Ponds in dead of night
Reflect the tears of the moon
Eyes of lunar deeps
Darkness dwells in the soul sewn
Everlasting lust that seeps.

FIREWORKS

Copious monsoon winds
Jet black heavens, us solus
The Clouds sang us hymns
Then the fireworks set ablaze
You peered into me in a daze.